FROM
EGG
TO
CHICKEN

Anita Ganeri

Heinemann
LIBRARY

www.heinemann.co.uk/library
Visit our website to find out more information about Heinem

To order:

 Phone 44 (0) 1865 888066

 Send a fax to 44 (0) 1865 314091

 Visit the Heinemann Bookshop at www.heinemann.co.uk/
our catalogue and order online.

First published in Great Britain by Heinemann Library,
Halley Court, Jordan Hill, Oxford OX2 8EJ, part of
Harcourt Education. Heinemann is a registered
trademark of Harcourt Education Ltd.

Editorial: Nancy Dickmann and Sarah Chappelow
Design: Ron Kamen and edesign
Picture Research: Ruth Blair and Kay Altwegg
Production: Helen McCreath

Originated by Modern Age
Printed and bound in China by South China
Printing Company

ISBN 0 431 05075 9
10 09 08 07 06
10 9 8 7 6 5 4 3 2 1

The British Library Cataloguing in Publication Data
Ganeri, Anita
From egg to chicken. - (How living things grow)
571.8'18625
A full catalogue record for this book is available from the
British Library.

Acknowledgements
The Publishers would like to thank the following for
permission to reproduce the following photographs:
Agripicture Images p. 5 (Peter Dean); Alamy pp. 6 (Tom
Gundelwein), 14 (Chris Warham); 16 (Juncal); Animals
Animals p. 17 (Jerry Cooke, Inc.); Ardea p. 10; Corbis p.
12 (Martin B. Withers/Frank Lane Picture Agency); FLPA
p. 27 (SDK Maslowski); Geoff Hansen p. 13; Harcourt
Education/Malcolm Harris pp. 11, 15, 20, 21, 22, 23, 24,
26; Getty Images p. 18 (photodisc); Holt Studios p. 7;
Photolibrary.com pp. 8, 9; Science Photo Library p. 25
(Kenneth H. Thomas); Superstock pp. 4 (Pixtal), 19
(Jerry Downs).

Cover photograph of a chicken and egg reproduced with
permission of Corbis/Brand X Pictures.

Illustrations: Martin Sanders

Every effort has been made to contact copyright holders
of any material reproduced in this book. Any omissions
will be rectified in subsequent printings if notice is given to
the publishers.

The paper used to print this book comes from
sustainable resources.

Contents

Words written in bold, **like this**, are explained in the glossary.

Have you ever seen a chicken?

A chicken is a kind of bird. It has feathers, wings, and a **beak**. People keep some chickens on farms. Eggs come from chickens.

These White Leghorn chickens live on a farm.

4

A female chicken is called a hen.

This chicken is a White Leghorn **hen**. You will learn how a chicken is born, grows up, has babies, gets old, and dies. This is the chicken's life cycle.

How does the hen's life cycle start?

Laying eggs

The **hen** starts life as an egg. The mother hen lays her eggs in a nest. There is a baby chicken in each egg. A baby chicken is called a **chick**.

The eggs are white and oval-shaped with hard shells.

The mother hen lays one egg a day. When she has laid about five eggs, she sits on them.

Chicks growing in the eggs need to keep warm.

When does the chick **hatch**?

Hatching out

Three weeks later, the mother **hen** hears a tapping sound. The eggs are starting to **hatch**.

Chicks are pecking through the eggshells

8

The **chick** uses her hard **beak** to crack the **eggshell**. Then she pushes her body out of her egg. Hatching is hard work!

What does the baby chick look like?

A new chick

The new **chick** has yellow feathers.
Her feathers are wet. But they
quickly dry out. The feathers keep
the chick warm.

A new chick has
damp feathers.

10

The feathers are soon dry and fluffy.

Soon all the other chicks in the nest have **hatched**. They start **cheeping** and looking around.

Does the chick stay close to her mother?

Off exploring

The **chick** is just one week old.
The chick stays close to her mother.
She follows her mother wherever
she goes.

Chicks feel safe if they stay close to their mother.

When she is older, the chick starts to explore the farmyard.

The young chicks have special food. It looks like breadcrumbs.

New feathers

As the **chicks** grow, they change colour. They have grown white feathers instead of their fluffy yellow ones.

The chick has grown and has new feathers.

By about six weeks old, the chick is much bigger. She starts to look more like her mother.

When does the chick leave her mother?

Leaving mother

The **chick** is now two months old. She is ready to leave her mother. The chick can now look after herself.

The chicks are big enough to explore by themselves.

The chicks nest in a wooden **hen**-*house at night.*

On the farm, she lives with the other chicks. They live in a **pen** in the farmyard. There is space to run about.

What does the chick eat?

17

Hungry chicks

The older **chicks** get special chick food to eat. The food helps the chicks to grow and stay healthy.

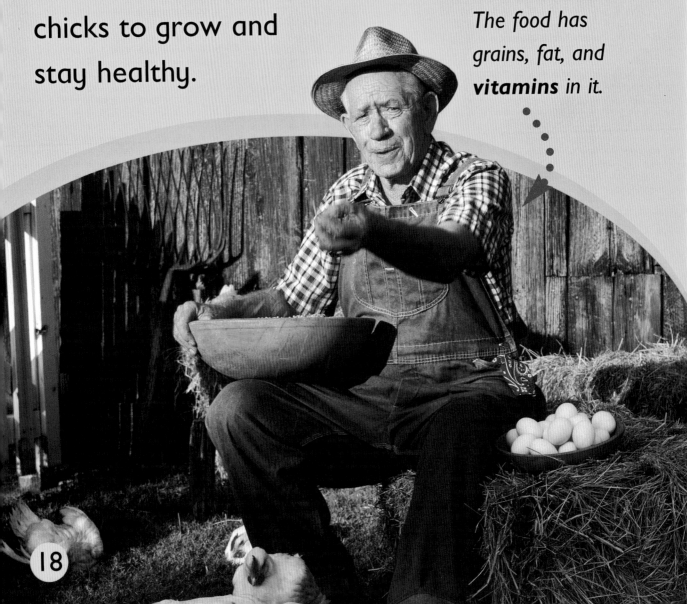

The food has grains, fat, and **vitamins** in it.

The chicks peck in the ground for juicy worms and insects to eat. Sometimes the farmer gives the chicks bits of fruit.

When does the chick lay her first egg?

First egg

The **chick** is five months old and almost fully grown. She is now called a **hen**.

One day, she sits in a quiet place and lays her first egg.

The hen has not **mated** so there are no chicks in her eggs. The farmer collects the eggs. These are the eggs we can buy in the shops and eat.

What is a male chicken called?

21

Cock-a-doodle-doo!

A male chicken is called a **cockerel**. This cockerel is about eight months old.

A cockerel looks and sounds different to a hen.

The cockerel looks after the **hens.** He chases away other cockerels. If a hen wanders off, he runs after her.

Time to mate

The **hen** is a year old. She is ready to **mate**. The **cockerel** mates with the hen.

After she mates, the hen can lay eggs with **chicks** in them. The chicks **hatch** after 21 days.

Staying safe

Sometimes, a hungry fox sneaks into the farmyard. Foxes steal **hens** to eat from the hen-house.

If she stays safe a hen can live until
she is about seven years old.
A **cockerel** can live until he is
about ten years old.

Life cycle of a chicken

1

Mother **hen**
lays eggs
(day 1)

2

Chick hatches
(21 days)

6

Hen and
cockerel mate
(1 year old)

3

Chick stays with
its mother
(1 week old)

5

Chick leaves
its mother
(2 months old)

4

Chick grows
white feathers
(6–7 weeks old)

28

Chicken map

tail

feathers

eyes

beak

feet

wings

Glossary

beak hard covering over a bird's mouth

cheeping sound a chick makes

chick baby chicken

cockerel male chicken

eggshell hard covering around an egg

hatch when an egg breaks open and a chick comes out

hen female chicken

mate when a male and female come together to make young

pen part of the farmyard where chickens live

vitamins goodness in food that keeps animals healthy

More books to read

Life as a Chicken, Vic Parker (Heinemann Library, 2003)

Nature's Patterns: Animal Life Cycles, Anita Ganeri
  (Heinemann Library, 2005)

The Life Cycle of a Chicken, Lisa Trumbauer (Capstone
  Press, 2002)

Websites to visit

Visit this site to find out more interesting facts about
chickens:
http://www.kiddyhouse.com/Farm/Chicken/Chicken.html

Index

Titles in the *How Living Things Grow* series include:

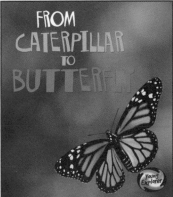 

Hardback   0 431 05079 1

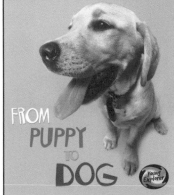

Hardback   0 431 05072 4

Hardback   0 431 05075 9

Hardback   0 431 05078 3

Hardback   0 431 05073 2

Hardback   0 431 05080 5

Hardback   0 431 05074 0

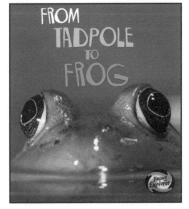

Hardback   0 431 05077 5

Find out about other Heinemann Library titles on our website www.heinemann.co.uk/library